RADICAL
FORGIVENESS

How to forgive and let
go of the pain attached to
remembering...

A.E. LEMUELIEL

Contact the author:
Email: ashastertrade@gmail.com

DEDICATION

To the Precious Holy Spirit who always reveals something unique and authentic with every case I handle. And makes every person I take through the 'forgiveness process' a new adventure for learning. Every person's case becomes a discovery as He keeps teaching me more about this life.

Also dedicated to my late mother, Paulina Amoah who never went to school but made it possible for me to be educated. I truly appreciate her sacrifices and her love to see me excel.

CONTENTS

INTRODUCTION

Many people want to forgive, but do not know how to do it effectively. This miracle book that changed my life will change yours too as you read. If you learn this act of true forgiveness that is shared in this book, you will live a life of complete peace, joy and fulfillment. If you have never been hurt before, this book is not for you. But if you have been hurt and you truly want to be free from the pain of those hurts, then you are holding in your hands a gift from God that will change your life forever.

After learning the act, you can practice it every morning to help you let go off the previous day's hurt and live a complete life of freedom. When we forgive, it's not just a mind game or imagination, but something happens to us on a deeper level. Our frequency changes and we are shifted unto a whole new level of enlightenment altogether. Let's get into it; your transformation begins now. Congratulations!

CHAPTER ONE

WHAT IS FORGIVENESS?

"In whom we have redemption through his blood, the forgiveness of sins, according to the riches of his grace,"

(Ephesians 1:7)

Forgiveness as translated in the verse above is from the Greek word "aphesis" which means release from bondage or imprisonment. It also means pardon or deliverance. This means that the opposite which is retribution or vengeance simply means to be in bondage or to be locked in prison. How many of us were or are locked up in one way or the other because of an offense? If you don't forgive, you are kept in prison for life. This account for the reason some people remain stagnant in life forever; never progressing and die without fulfilling any purpose. It's all because they couldn't let go of their past mistakes or forgive those who hurt them badly. You are meant for worldly impact. The world needs your impact hence you cannot afford to lock yourself in a prison while your talents and gifts are needed.

THE BENEFITS OF FORGIVENESS

Being unforgiving poisons the body. It's like drinking poison and thinking another person would suffer for it. The world doesn't work that way. When you check your chemistries in a laboratory, you will get some good result. However if before the test you remember the person you have not forgiven and become very bitter and angry about what they put you through, the result will change. Where did that poison come from? Your own cells manufactured the poison to destroy the body. This is why you must let go and forgive everything.

1. Forgiveness sets you free, not the offender

> *"So likewise shall my heavenly Father do also unto you, if ye from your hearts forgive not everyone his brother their trespasses,"*
>
> *(Matthew 18:35)*

Remaining in the prison of your mind and blaming another person for the cause of your pains is easy, but you need to break out of that prison. The Bible says whosoever the son makes free shall be free indeed. You have been set free by Jesus already. The truth is that when you forgive, something happens to your soul and mind that is higher than the physical. There is a shift in frequency. You move unto a higher dimension of life. Your soul becomes clean enough to receive the light of God. Your energy field becomes clearer, and purer, attracting more light around you. An unforgiving heart brings darkness around you that attract demons to hide in there and torment you. These demons speak to your mind and give you all sorts of negative thoughts, such as to commit suicide or curse the person who caused you pain. In the spiritual realm, these demons use you as their refuse dump; they dump all sorts of bad things into your life.

2. Forgiveness clears your path for heavenly ascension

> *"Blessed are the pure in heart: for they shall see God,"*
>
> *(Matthew 5:8)*

One day I was in a trance ascending to heaven, then I realized something was holding me down so I asked myself what it was. Just then, I knew within me, it was my unforgiving heart. So I took time to forgive that person then I started ascending again. An unforgiving heart will stunt your growth in Christ. Forgiveness will speed up your ascension and open certain portals for you in Heaven.

3. Forgiveness Activates Creativity

Being unforgiving will inhibit your creativity. A scientific research that was conducted proved that when a person goes through radical forgiveness, his brain wave is tuned like that of a monk who has meditated for several years. The research also says people who are able to forgive produce more dopamine—the chemical responsible for mood elevation in the brain. Forgiveness can improve your mood and make you more optimistic over the long run.

Radical forgiveness shifts your brain wave onto alpha frequency—the frequency responsible for creative imagination; the brain wave of an artist under inspiration.

4. Forgiveness makes your face shine

> "This then is the message which we have heard of him, and declare unto you, that God is light, and in him is no darkness

at all. If we say that we have fellowship with him, and walk in darkness, we lie, and do not the truth: But if we walk in the light, as he is in the light, we have fellowship one with another, and the blood of Jesus Christ his Son cleanses us from all sin,"

(1John 1:5-7)

We are children of light and when we forgive we show forth our light. We then operate on the level of God consciousness. Repeat this: *"as Christ is, so am I in this world, and I have forgiven all who will ever wrong me of all their sins. I love to do so and I've done it so easily."*

Some people think that if we don't forgive, God will not forgive us. In matters concerning heavenly court and justice, this is true when man is seeking justice from God. Matthew 6: 14-15 KJV says, *"For if we forgive men their trespasses your heavenly father will also forgive you, but if ye forgive not men their trespasses neither will your father forgive your trespasses."*

However concerning matters of eternal redemption, God has already forgiven all believers of their sins. The Sins we will commit in the future and that of the past has already been forgiven. Why would God hold grudges in His heart against a man who chooses not forgive his fellow man? I think God would live in bitterness looking at the number of people who still hold things against their neighbors.

Ephesians 4: 32 says, *"And be ye kind one to another, tenderhearted, forgiving one another, even as God for Christ's sake hath forgiven you."*

Because of the death of Christ, your past sins and future sins have been forgiven already. When you forgive those who genuinely hurt you, you are elevated, your frequency shifts to the level which you originally belong to in Christ. It's in forgiveness that God makes the world fear him, not in punishment.

Psalm 130: 4 says, *"but there is forgiveness with thee that thou mayest be feared."*

When we genuinely forgive people, they begin to fear us. The Bible says that when Stephen was brought to be stoned, he was full of the Holy Ghost. I believe Stephen had a forgiving heart that was why. And the Bible says his face shone like that of an angel.

Acts 7:60 says, *"And Stephen, while he was being stoned, made prayer to God, saying, Lord Jesus, take my spirit. And going down on his knees, he said in a loud voice, Lord, do not make them responsible for this sin. And when he had said this, he went to his rest"(BBE).*

Stephen's face shone like that of an Angel as he spoke.

Acts 6:15 says. *"And all those who were in the Sanhedrin, looking at him, saw that his face was like the face of an angel" (BBE)*

Stephen emulated the Lord Jesus when he was hanged on the cross; he sought forgiveness for the people.

Luke 23:34 says, *"Then said Jesus, Father, forgive them; for they know not what they do. And they parted his raiment, and cast lots."*

So when you forgive, you become radiant and full of the Holy Ghost.

THINK ON THESE
1. Forgiveness sets you free, and not the offender.
2. Forgiveness clears your path for heavenly ascension.
3. Forgiveness Activates Creativity.
4. Forgiveness makes your face shine

CHAPTER TWO

AUTHORITY TO FORGIVE SINS

"Whose soever sins ye remit, they are remitted unto them; and whose soever sins ye retain, they are retained"
(John 20:23 KJV)

UNDERSTANDING JOHN 20:23

"Whose soever sins ye remit, they are remitted unto them; and whose soever sins ye retain, they are retained,"
(John 20:23 KJV).

When the Lord made this statement, he had resurrected from the dead and was in His glorious body. The preceding verse says that he breathed upon them, the Holy Ghost. Verse 21 says, *"Then said Jesus to them again, Peace be unto you: as my Father hath sent me, even so send I you."*

Jesus was speaking in reference to the place He has placed us. He brought us to the place where He gave us the authority to forgive sins on earth.

The Jews believed that only God can forgive sins.

> *"And, behold, they brought to him a man sick of the palsy, lying on a bed: and Jesus seeing their faith said unto the sick of the palsy; Son, be of good cheer; thy sins be forgiven thee,"*
>
> *(Matthew 9:2)*

> *The next verse says "And, behold, certain of the scribes said within themselves, this man blasphemeth,"*
>
> *(Matthew 9:3)*

So in verse 6 Jesus responded to their thoughts and said, *"But that ye may know that the Son of man hath power on earth to forgive sins, (then saith he to the sick of the palsy,) Arise, take up thy bed, and go unto thine house. And he arose, and departed to his house. But when the multitudes saw it, they marvelled, and glorified God, which had given such power unto men."* (Matthew 9:6-8).

When you read the above scripture carefully, you will notice that Jesus was proving that He has the authority to forgive sins by commanding the sick man to be healed.

Jesus wanted them to know that the Son of man has power on earth to forgive sins; so he proved it by commanding the sick man to arise from his sick bed. In other words, the power to command the sick to be made well was a proof that He had authority to forgive sins.

When Jesus was raised from the dead, He gave us that authority to forgive sins on earth. The word translated as "Power" in the verse above is the Greek word "exousia" which means "delegated authority" It also means power of choice.

So this means that the new creation man has the power of choice to forgive men their sins, and heaven will forgive them. We have been given the authority to forgive sins on earth. Jesus was not saying that if someone wrongs you and you hold it against them it will be held against them. Remember, if you hold it against them, another believer may meet them and say to them "your sins have been forgiven thee" and they will be forgiven in heaven. When Jesus was sent by the father, He gave Him the authority to forgive sins on earth in the father's stead. Same way, Jesus has given us the authority to forgive sins on the earth in His stead when He sent us. For example the policeman has been given the authority to arrest and forgive people on the street. If a policeman forgives you of an offence you made on the street, the government has forgiven you.

Remember that the authority to forgive sins was only given in addition to the command to preach the gospel. So in effect, it's an ambassadorial authority.

James the Apostle backed this believe.

> "And the prayer of faith will save those being sick, and the Lord will raise him up. And if he may have committed sin, it will be forgiven him. Confess to one another the deviations from the Law, and pray for one another, that you may be healed. Very strong is a righteous petition, being made effective,"
>
> (James 5:15-16 LITV).

So you can pray for forgiveness for me, and I can do same for you. And it doesn't matter whether I offended you or another person did.

Remember John the Baptist? The people went to him to be baptized, while confessing their sins.

> "Then Jerusalem and all Judea went out to him, and all the neighborhood of the Jordan, and were baptized by him in the Jordan, confessing their sins,"
>
> (Matthew 3:5-6).

Who did they confess their sins to? It was John the Baptist of course. If not, they could have as well confessed in their homes, and God would hear them.

The people might have had some believe that John was a righteous man and that he had an authority from God to lead them to receive forgiveness of sins.

But remember that Jesus said He that is least in the kingdom is greater than John.

> "For I say to you, among those born of a woman, no prophet is greater than John the Baptist. But the least one in the

kingdom of God is greater than he is,"
                              (Luke 7:28 KJV).

Paul the Apostle said he also forgive sins.

> *"I will forgive anyone you forgive. Yes, for your sake and with Christ as my witness, I have forgiven whatever needed to be forgiven,"*
>
> *(2 Corinthians 2:10)*

Remember these people didn't offend Paul directly, but he forgave them on behalf of those they offended, with Jesus as his witness.

Remember that as believers, we are not permitted to hold on to sins of people except only on the account of preaching the gospel; that is only when we are carrying out an evangelistic duty.

> *"And whosoever shall not receive you, nor hear you, when ye depart thence, shake off the dust under your feet for a testimony against them. Verily I say unto you, It shall be more tolerable for Sodom and Gomorrah in the day of judgment, than for that city,"*
>
> *(Mark 6:11).*

The question now is, if I don't forgive the one who offended me, what happens to them? The truth is, that person may have confessed that sin to another believer who in turn asked for forgiveness for him through prayer, and God had forgiven him already. You are the one that would be holding that hurt in your heart, but before God, that person has been forgiven when that brother asked for forgiveness for him.

Now let's ask, "Can we forgive sin?" Yes with Jesus Christ as our witness.

THINK ON THESE

- He brought us to the place where He gave us the authority to forgive sins on earth.

- Remember that the authority to forgive sins was only given in addition to the command to preach the gospel. So in effect, it's an ambassadorial authority.

- Remember that as believers, we are not permitted to withhold sins of people except only on the account of preaching the gospel; that is only when we are carrying out an evangelistic duty.

CHAPTER THREE

WHY MUST WE FORGIVE?

"And hope maketh not ashamed; because the love of God is shed abroad in our hearts by the Holy Ghost which is given unto us."

(Romans 5:5)

Anger, resentment, and hatred are all poison you drink expecting someone else to die when you refuse to forgive. But that is not how God created the world; when you drink something poisonous, you are the one to be affected. Anger and bitterness affects the health of your liver. It poisons your body and places a lot of stress on your liver. So when you are filled with bitterness it's only going to hurt you and not the other person. Forgiveness brings to you peace of mind and heart. Without peace, there is no prosperity. You must forgive because you are united with God, and that it's your nature to forgive—to love doing it and to do it at any time. You must forgive because the love of God is already shed abroad in your heart by the Holy Ghost.

Romans 5:5 says, *"And hope maketh not ashamed; because the love of God is shed abroad in our hearts by the Holy Ghost which is given unto us."*

Most of the people who hurt you were once your loved ones; people who genuinely loved you. Even if they were pretenders you have to forgive them because you are one with God, and you are made in His likeness. Don't limit yourself by thinking of yourself as a mere man.

THINK ON THESE

- Without peace, there is no prosperity.

- Most of the people who hurt you were once your loved ones; people who genuinely loved you.

CHAPTER FOUR

RADICAL FORGIVENESS

*"But I say unto you, Love your enemies,
bless them that curse you, do good to them
that hate you, and pray for them which
despitefully use you, and persecute you,"*
(Matthew 5:44)

Radical forgiveness is total forgiveness that must end in loving the person who hurt you. In radical forgiveness, God wants you to forgive the person and then love them genuinely as well. Love them again. Luke 6: 35 says, *"But love ye your enemies, and do good, and lend, hoping for nothing again; and your reward shall be great, and ye shall be the children of the Highest: for he is kind unto the unthankful and to the evil."*

Note that I am not saying you should unite with the person and rekindle the relationship, but to go your separate ways without feeling pain whenever you remember the person. For some people, the best way to show love is to go your separate ways yet holding nothing against them.

THE TYPE OF SIN THAT CANNOT BE FORGIVEN

The Bible says when you sin against the Holy Ghost, it shall not be forgiven. Peter demonstrated the judgment of God when Ananias and his wife lied to the Holy Ghost.

> But Peter said, Ananias, why hath Satan filled thine heart to lie to the Holy Ghost, and to keep back part of the price of the land?
>
> Whiles it remained, was it not thine own? and after it was sold, was it not in thine own power? why hast thou conceived this thing in thine heart? thou hast not lied unto men, but unto God.
>
> And Ananias hearing these words fell down, and gave up the ghost: and great fear came on all them that heard these things.
>
> And the young men arose, wound him up, and carried him out, and buried him.
>
> (Acts 5:3-6)

In this instance, Peter had to make God's judgment prevail for the people to fear God. Some situations require the judgment of God to prevail.

In Acts 12, the Bible tells us Herod killed James, and took Peter also. But the Church prayed earnestly for him. Now when the Angel rescued Peter, Herod also received God's judgment.

> *"Immediately an angel of the Lord struck him down, because he did not give God the glory, and he was eaten by worms and breathed his last."*
>
> *(Acts 12:23) ESV*

WHAT YOU NEED TO FORGIVE

You need to forgive these entities.

1. Forgive yourself for your past mistakes, because they happened to teach you about life.
   forgive your childhood; your younger self
   forgive yourself for the bad choices you made by ignoring the signals. Even if the person was 99% wrong, you were 1% wrong too, so admit your own fault.

2. Forgive your children of the little things they did wrong and even the biggest mistake that cost you a lot of money.

3. Forgive your parents for the bad choices they made of which you bear some consequences. It could be your parents are divorced and because of that you were brought up by a single parent or a relative.

4. Forgive those whose death may have cost you a lot to bear all alone in life.

5. Forgive your boss, teacher, colleague, etc. Forgive even the waiter who was disrespectful to you, forgive that driver who insulted you on the road.

6. For those who feel God has disappointed them they need to forgive themselves for holding such a thought. God never disappoints. They need to ask for forgiveness.

7. Forgive people who genuinely hurt you. It could be a robber who attacked you on the road or broke into your house, or your colleague who made you lose your job.

8. 8. Forgive your enemies. This is because

most of the people you call enemies were once your loved ones. They were once your friends. They became enemies because they betrayed your love or disappointed you. You have the power to live in enlightenment above human limitations by forgiving.

THINK ON THESE
1. Forgive yourself
2. Forgive your children
3. Forgive your parents
4. Forgive those who died
5. Forgive your boss, teacher, colleague
6. Forgive people who genuinely hurt you.
7. Forgive your enemies

MANIFESTATIONS OF UNFORGIVENESS
Being unforgiving manifests in the body with many symptoms including chronic lower back pain. When you harbor past wounds, they keep drawing you back and manifests itself in the body as a disease. Sometimes it manifests in the form of a liver disease, because anger and resentment poison the body. You may develop an angry personality.

CHRONIC WAIST PAIN DISAPPEAR AFTER FORGIVENESS

There was a time I had chronic waste pain which wouldn't go away. I did all I could; I went to see a physiotherapist, but after the session it went away temporarily, but as soon as I got home, it appeared again. It was when I took myself through the radical forgiveness model as described in later chapters that I realized I was holding on to the pain caused by people I loved who betrayed me instead of supporting me. I realized that I was holding on to a "Nobody supports me" mindset. So I willingly forgave that person and just after that, the waist pain went away.

INCREDIBLE HAPPENINGS

Sis. Anita A., a very good friend of mine, went through the radical forgiveness model and after that incredible happenings, the first thing that she noticed was that, chronic headache disappeared, then back pain also disappeared, and pains in her legs all went away immediately. Her spiritual eyes opened and she saw herself before the throne of God in heaven and she found herself asking God some questions. After the process, she confessed to me that if she is to rate the process on a scale of 1 to 10, she would love to give something above 50.

SWOLLEN FEET HEALED

I was teaching on this topic on Clubhouse, and after that I took them through a short meditative session to scan their energy field and then forgive. There were many beautiful experiences. One of it was a woman who had a swollen foot, and was really weak. After the process, the swell around her foot disappeared, and she received energy to do series of house chores without any issue. The energy she had received was overwhelming. One lady said to me, "I thought I had already forgiven them, I didn't know I still held on to it." She was getting angry as she recalled the scene to mind, and it was a sign that she still held on to the past. But after the process, she was completely free.

Many people say that using this model has made them practically free from the effects of the negative comments of people. Negative comments and people's reactions don't affect them anymore because they choose what to allow into their inner most being.

MORNING FORGIVENESS

"Be ye angry, and sin not: let not the sun go down upon your wrath,"
> *(Ephesians 4:26).*

Practicing morning forgiveness simply makes you roll off the burdens of the previous day. You must not be boiling with anger for 24 hours. Hurts and resentments from the past taints the light field around us.

Bathing your energy field with radical forgiveness will cause the light of God to flow through you unhindered. The negative reactions of people towards you stays with you and that is why you need to forgive everything; not only people but as much as possible even things. You need to forgive the waiter who misbehaved towards you at the restaurant. You need to forgive your wife or your husband for what they did the previous day. Everything that happened to you in the previous day need to be forgiven.

The human aura is the refraction of the light of the human spirit through the prism of the human body. Peter said that we are lively stones. *"Ye also, as lively stones, are built up a spiritual house, an holy priesthood, to offer up spiritual sacrifices, acceptable to God by Jesus Christ," (1 Peter 2:5KJV).*

The human body is a likened to a stone prism. When the light from your spirit flows through it unhindered, the aura you produce becomes bright.

Hurts and resentments from the past taints the light field around us.

We are surrounded by a field of God's glory and this is referred to as aura. This glory or aura can be darkened by hurts and bitterness and this may hinder our prayers from ascending as pure incense.

Therefore you need to bath your aura through radical forgiveness. Being unforgiving creates darkness in our aura. Stones are formed when clay is subjected under high intensity of pressure and heat. The Bible says we are lively stones, and that means that we refract the light coming from within us and this produces the aura. Your aura must retain the glory of God and keep it. Under pure light of Christ, all the dark fields within you are revealed. This is why you must forgive, in order to clean up the glory of God in you completely.

THINK ON THESE

- Bathing your energy field with radical forgiveness will cause the light of God to flow through you unhindered

- Hurts and resentments from the past taints the light field around us.

- Practicing morning forgiveness simply makes you roll off the burdens of the previous day.

CHAPTER FIVE

FORGIVING AND FORGETTING

"I, even I, am he that blotteth out thy transgressions for mine own sake, and will not remember thy sins,"

(Isaiah 43:25)

CAN WE FORGIVE AND FORGET?

Is it actually possible to forget a hurtful event as if it never happened? If there's a technique to actually do that I think we will go for that. But what does the Bible say about forgetting? Let's see God's perspective on forgiveness since we are His children. We are one with the Father, the Son, and the Holy Spirit.

"I, even I, am he that blotteth out thy transgressions for mine own sake, and will not remember thy sins,"

(Isaiah 43:25)

In the verse above, we see God saying for His own sake, He blotted out our transgressions and will not remember our sins. When you choose to blot out the sins of people who hurt you and let go of the pain, it's for your own sake.

God has the ability to choose what he wants to remember and simply chooses to forget what he wants to forget, but that does not mean the event didn't happen. Transgression means to traverse from the assigned pathway destined for you. It means to miss the way; it also means to trespass.

Sometimes the human brain can automatically erase the memory because it doesn't want to remember past traumatic events. It can be that severe that you don't only lose memory of things, but also people you have a meaningful relationship with. A typical example is the case of a woman whose house was raided by robbers. They shot her husband and smashed her baby's head on the wall in front of her. Instantly, her brain shut down. She couldn't remember anything of her past again, to the extent that she even forgot her own relatives. This is the brain's own activity and this is a very difficult case. It's the brain's mechanism of protecting her; making her survive on earth.

Now, when I say forgive and forget, it is not this automatic mechanism of brain that I expect. I am talking about forgiving and changing the meaning attached to the event. That doesn't mean you will forget the event, however, the power that the event has on you will be broken completely because, the meaning attached to it has been broken.

> *"Change the meaning attached to the event and get the true meaning of why that happened"*

WHY DO WE GET SO OFFENDED BY WHAT PEOPLE DO TO US?

It's simply because of the meaning attached to their actions. If the meaning is not changed, you all carry those hurts for years and never recover. You will never be able to really forgive the person if the meaning is not changed.

Remember Jesus was humiliated, scourged, and crucified naked, but was never offended by the actions of the people because the meaning attached to their actions was stronger than the act itself.

What their actions meant to Him was that, they are killing me so that with my blood I can pay for the sins of the whole world, and through that I would be buried, rise, and attain the name above all names.

> So on the cross Jesus said, "Father forgive
> them; for they know not what they do,"
> (Luke 20:34)

If we do not make the reason of the actions of people better and stronger than the pain itself, we will not be able to fully forgive people. God says He will blot out our trespasses and will choose not to remember our sins. That means, He will remove the pain attached to the actions. An action in itself may not be sinful, but the reason behind it is what makes it sinful. In other words, God will remember the action but will forget what makes it a sinful act. So that means He will not remember our sins anymore.

THE BEAUTY OF PAIN
We all have some scars on our skin in one way or the other. All of us have been wounded

physically before. Even babies are wounded in the first week they are born by a nurse, laboratory scientist, or phlebotomist pushing a needle into their skin and taking some blood samples for analysis.

Scars can be very beautiful, and can be very disgusting depending on the cause.

> "But Thomas, one of the twelve, called Didymus, was not with them when Jesus came. The other disciples therefore said unto him, We have seen the Lord. But he said unto them, Except I shall see in his hands the print of the nails, and put my finger into the print of the nails, and thrust my hand into his side, I will not believe.
>
> And after eight days again his disciples were within, and Thomas with them: then came Jesus, the doors being shut, and stood in the midst, and said, Peace be unto you.
>
> Then saith he to Thomas, Reach hither thy finger, and behold my hands; and reach hither thy hand, and thrust it into my side: and be not faithless, but believing."
>
> (John 20:24-27)

In the scripture above, we see how Jesus still carries in His glorious body the scars from the cross. He does not deny the event on the cross ever happening. He is showing us the beauty of a scar. Scars are beautiful and has its own prize if it was for a worthy course. Our Lord carries the scar from the cross to heaven, and presently still bears it.

There was a time I was on Mount Olives, Nkawkaw in the Eastern part of my home country Ghana. I saw the Lord physically walking towards me. The mountain was high and I was someway close to the top. As he walked towards me, I could still see the hole in His feet very wide and a beam of light shining from it.

Jesus our Lord has completely forgiven those who killed Him on the cross. In fact, He did it while still on the cross, but He still carries the scars. The reason for those scars is stronger than the pain He went through.

Beloved, I don't know who has hurt you so badly or what you are holding on to that you think you cannot let go. It's true they hurt you so badly. It cannot be as bad as what they did to Jesus on the cross. If only you can change the reason attached to the event, then will you be free from that pain. And that is what am going to show you.

Yes, they hurt you so badly, everyone knows. It may have even come into the news and everyone knows about it. But you can't remain here. Nobody has the power to bring your life to a standstill or keep you in a prison. You have the right to blame them for your misfortune, but you can also be like our Lord by rising above the hurts, because the reason for the hurts was a good one. So instead of saying "he hurt me badly", you can say, "I learned forgiveness; I learned about life; I matured as a person". What is the reason attached to those hurts? You need to change it before you can transcend above it.

Therefore, make the reason why they hurt you stronger than the pain or wound, then the scar would still look beautiful on you. Tell that person, "you hurt me badly, you caused me pain, but I have matured to become a better person. If it wasn't so, I may never have gotten a certain wisdom." You may have suffered loss of a relationship, or many things, but that has produced a strong personality in you.

SAME EVENTS, BUT DIFFERENT REASON SO DIFFERENT RESULTS

This is a true story of a girl in India whose parents wanted to abort her when she was conceived. When the mother conceived her, they thought they didn't need that baby so they tried all sorts of procedures to terminate the pregnancy but didn't succeed. So eventually, they gave birth to the girl. Now at a young age, they told the girl, "When we had you, we thought we were not ready for you so we tried all sorts of nasty things to abort you but we didn't succeed. We believe you are here for a special reason and that you are going to be a great person. This girl grew up to be one of the best lawyers the country has produced, because she heard a good reason for the actions of her parents.

Another person was also told that her parents wanted to abort her when she was conceived and her life has become a disaster. She built the belief that she was worthless, and if her own parents didn't want her from the beginning, then who would want her?

She goes through life looking miserable, building no relationships, because the reason for her parent's action was wrong.

Whatever reason you give to your mind, it will absorb it without any judgment; whether good or bad, your mind will get a hold of it.

Why don't you change the reason for the actions of people and completely change your life?

A CEO WHO WAS DUPED

There is another story of a CEO of a company whose partner duped him and stole huge sums of money from the company.

When the CEO found out about this fraudulent act, the partner threatened the life of the man and his family. This made the CEO very bitter about the situation and their relationship eventually ended. However this CEO decided to forgive the man. He had a hard time forgiving him, but eventually he had to be empathetic about the whole situation. He said to himself, "maybe that guy had bad parenting, or maybe his wife was in the hospital, or perhaps his children needed some good education, or perhaps his family was poor, or maybe a family member was needing help from him so badly." So this man managed to forgive his partner. The following year was the most successful year of the company.

There's no point in holding a wrong meaning to why people hurt you. Since it has never served you good over the years, it will not change if you continue with that belief. It's time to change your life. Change that reason, and the belief will change. Develop empathy for those who hurt you by finding a reason for which they had to do what they did. And determine that what they did has no power to destroy your life, but has given you the power to rise above that challenge.

THINK ON THESE

- You will never be able to really forgive the person if the reason for their action is not changed.

- Change the meaning attached to the event and get the true meaning of why that happened.

CHAPTER SIX

HOW TO FORGIVE

*Peter came up to Jesus and asked him,
"Lord, how many times may my brother
sin against me and I have to forgive him?
Seven times?"*

(Matthew 18:21)

God's word is the answer to every life's issue. It will be very easy to forgive if you are operating from the realm of God. This is the realm of perfection in love. God is love and we are born of Him; therefore, you and I are love personified. Walking in bitterness and not being forgiving means we have forgotten who we really are and we are walking in a lower standard of life.

1. **Be specific about what you are forgiving.** Being specific is the first step to your freedom. You have to know who you are forgiving and what you want to forgive—the specific thing.

2. The Holy Ghost is our help

> *"Likewise the Spirit also helpeth our infirmities: for we know not what we should pray for as we ought: but the Spirit itself maketh intercession for us with groanings which cannot be uttered,"*
>
> 3. *(Romans 8:26)*

To completely forgive, you will need the help of the Holy Ghost. Pray and ask God to help you forgive the people who have really hurt you. The Holy Spirit knows the motives of people. Sometimes the people don't even know what they did to us hurt us so badly. But the Bible says that the Holy Spirit will lead you into all truth. The truth behind that action will be revealed by the Holy Ghost. What was really in their hearts will be revealed. Ask the Holy Spirit to help you let go of the pain from the hurt, and decide to operate in God's love.

HOW MANY TIMES MUST WE FORGIVE?

God wants us to live one day at a time. The Message Bible explains Matthew 6:34 as "Give your entire attention to what God is doing right now, and don't get worked up about what may or may not happen tomorrow. God will help you deal with whatever hard things come up when the time comes." When God wants us to forgive, it must be now! Don't say I will do it tomorrow.

In Matthew 18:21 Peter came up to Jesus and asked him, *"Lord, how many times may my brother sin against me and I have to forgive him? Seven times?"* (Mat 18:21)

> *Then Jesus said to him, "I tell you, not just seven times, but 77 times!"*
> *(Mathew 18:22)*

Jesus is not saying you should count seventy-seven in your life time to forgive your brother of his sins. He meant that when the day is over your counting is over; the next day, you have to start counting afresh. If someone offends you today, forgive him/her seventy-seven times the sins he does today. Nobody can offend you seventy-seven times in a day. However, the next day, if he offends you seventy-seven times, forgive all.

Jesus wants us to completely forgive on daily basis and not carry hurts into the next day. How many times must we forgive a person of their sins in a day? The answer is simple, seventy-seven times (77×).

PRAY FOR YOUR ENEMIES

> *"But I say to you, love your enemies, and pray for those who persecute you, so that you will become children of your Father in heaven, because he makes his sun rise on both evil and good people, and he lets rain fall on the righteous and the unrighteous."*
>
> *(Matthew 5:44-45)*

To walk in complete forgivingness, you need to apply the word of God no matter how difficult it may be. God wants us to love our enemies. Then he shows us how to love them; by blessing and praying for them. Most of the people who are now your enemies were once your loved ones. Jesus says love them. Have compassion on them and pray for them. Bless them. If there is difficulty in loving them, you need to pray for them by blessing them every day till there is no hatred for them left in your heart.

When you pray for your enemies, the first thing God will bless them with is the revelation of what they have done. Speak well of them instead of evil. Remember only the good things they did for you; remember only that and not their evil.

THINK ON THESE

1. Be specific about what you are forgiving.

2. The Holy Ghost is our help.

CHAPTER SEVEN

THE PROCESS OF COMPLETELY FORGIVING

Sometimes you may think you have completely forgiven until you hear the person's name, then you become offended. That means even though you have forgiven, the incident still hurts you. This technique is to help you completely let go of the pain from the hurt and release the person into love.

PRACTICING FORGIVENESS

The process is simple; you have to sit down straight or lie down with your eyes closed, and imagine the light from heaven falling on your body. Let this light move through your body to the earth. This light is the love light from God.

In your mind's eye, you will notice the darkness in certain portions around your body. This is the field around you. If there are dark portions, just ask yourself, "Who do I need to forgive?" The name of the person will come to you readily. So you go back to REVIEW what they did to you.

VERY IMPORTANT: **YOU ARE NOT RELIVING THE EXPERIENCE, YOU ARE ONLY REVIEWING IT.**

As you review it, ask yourself why they did that to you. Develop empathy for them. Maybe they didn't know they were hurting you. Maybe they couldn't bear the pain they were experiencing that is why they left you. You need to be bold about it, and face the situation. Don't just say you don't want to remember. You are only reviewing it, not reliving it; just like Jesus will review the events of the cross to remind Himself of the meaning of the cross. Could it be that the person wanted to protect himself that's why they did what they did? Could it be that the person was in a dire need of money to help a family member that is why they stole from you?"

Ponder over why they did that to you. If you feel telling them your peace of mind will make you okay, just say it then after that release them into love and forgiveness.

Now imagine the person is in front of you; hug them, and tell them how much you love them, and tell them that you have completely forgiven them. Then imagine the Lord Jesus in front of you; hold the hand of the person, and stand in front of the Lord Jesus. Put your hands around the neck of the person and imagine Jesus hugging both of you. See all the darkness disappear, and the two of you being filled with the light of Jesus. You, the person and Jesus are full of the light; you are light beings.

If you find it difficult to do this, you can check out my hypnosis for forgiveness on the Conscious Christian Network channel on YouTube and download the meditation guide for forgiveness.

EARLY MORNING FORGIVENESS

We are all energetic beings and throughout our day to day activities, we are interacting with energies. When you meet an angry person, you may interact with his/her frequency. You may absorb his /her frequency without knowing. The waiter who treated you harshly needs to be forgiven, the driver who insulted you needs to be forgiven, the harsh words of your wife or husband needs to be forgiven. The mistakes you did the previous day needs to be forgiven. The opportunities you didn't take needs to be forgiven.

When we forgive the previous day's events, we make the new day a clean sheet for which we can rewrite a new story.

Practicing early morning forgiveness will completely transform your day.

NOW BLESS YOUR DAY – MORNING BLESSING (BALL OF LIGHT)

DO THIS AFTER THE FORGIVENESS –

Close your eyes and imagine God's light falling on your body. Imagine you are holding a ball of light with your two hands. This light is Love. Bless your day with anything you wish to see by speaking over the light. Let it come from your heart. For example, "I bless my day with beautiful partnership, I bless my day with 500 Dollars, I bless my day with opportunities to make 1000 dollars today, etc."

After that, push this ball of light into your heart and imagine the light growing brighter, then expand it beyond your body and spread it into space. Then release words of life; bless your life, your day, etc.

You will notice that every word you spoke will begin to manifest in your life.

THINK ON THESE
1. When you meet an angry person, you may interact with his/her frequency. You may absorb his /her frequency without knowing.
2. When we forgive the previous day, we make the new day a clean sheet for which we can rewrite a new story.
3. Practicing early morning forgiveness will completely transform your day.
4. Do Early Morning Forgiveness

5. Now bless your day – morning blessing (ball of light)

THE PROCESS IS SIMPLIFIED

1. Sit down straight, or lie down upright with closed eyes and imagine the light from heaven falling on your body.

2. Let this light move through your body into the earth. This light is the love light from God.

3. In your mind's eye, you will notice the darkness in certain portions around your body. This is the field around you. If there are dark portions, just ask yourself, "Who do I need to forgive?" The name of the person will come to you readily. So you go back to REVIEW what they did to you.

4. As you review it, ask yourself why they did that to you. Develop empathy for them.

5. Ponder over why they did that to you. If you feel telling them your peace of mind will make you okay, just say it then after that release them into love and forgiveness.

6. Now bless your day–morning blessing (Become conscious of the light- ball of light blessing)

CHAPTER EIGHT

DEALING WITH JEALOUSY

THE REAL MEANING OF JEALOUSY

Is jealousy really evil? What does the Bible say about Jealousy?

In this section after you have finished reading this, you will never be Jealous of anyone in your life again and you will rather use Jealousy as a tool for advancement and fulfillment of God's dream for your life.

WE SERVE A JEALOUS GOD

> "For thou shalt worship no other god: for the LORD, whose name is Jealous, is a jealous God,"
>
> (Exodus 34:14KJV)

The verse above says God's name is Jealous. Wow! God is a Jealous God. Jealousy is not evil, it's the nature of God, and God uses it as His name. The Jealousy of God is likened to fire; it burns like fire. He does not want any graven images to take His glory; He doesn't share His glory with idols. Deuteronomy 4:24 says, *"for the Lord thy God is a consuming fire, even a jealous God."*

Ezekiel 36:5 says, *"Therefore thus saith the Lord GOD; surely in the fire of my jealousy have I spoken against the residue of the heathen, and against all Idumea, which have appointed my land into their possession with the joy of all their heart, with despiteful minds, to cast it out for a prey."*

Zephaniah 3:8 says *"...for the earth shall be devoured with the fire of jealousy."*

The jealousy of God is called "Godly jealousy". We as believers need to walk in Godly jealousy, fulfilling the demands of God upon our lives. Throughout scripture and history, men who were driven by Godly jealousy fulfilled greater works in God. We must pray for Godly jealousy to fill us all.

Elijah was driven by Godly jealousy to stand for God in 1 Kings 18:21.

"And Elijah came unto all the people, and said, 'How long halt ye between two opinions? if the LORD be God, follow him: but if Baal, then follow him.' And the people answered him not a word,"

(1 Kings 18:21)

He slew all the prophets of Bal because he was driven by godly Jealousy.

"And Elijah said unto them, Take the prophets of Baal; let not one of them escape. And they took them: and Elijah brought them down to the brook Kishon, and slew them there,"

(1 Kings 18:40)

David said in Ps 69:9 that *"the zeal of thine house hath eaten me up…"*

The word translated as zeal here is "qinah" which means "jealousy". It means he was saying, *"The jealousy of your house has eaten me up."*

In John 2:13 to the verses after, we see Jesus being driven by Godly jealousy. He went into the temple on Passover and saw people buying and selling in the temple. Jesus was driven by Godly jealousy to drive them all out of the temple.

"Then he told those who were selling the doves, "Take these things out of here! Stop making my Father's house a marketplace!"

(John 2:16 ISV)

"And his disciples remembered that it was written, the zeal of thine house hath eaten me up"

(John 2:17, Psalm 69:9)

Without Godly jealousy we cannot go on missions; we cannot win souls, we cannot save people from the kingdom of darkness. Why do we win souls? Because we are driven by Godly Jealousy. We cannot stand it when Satan is populating his kingdom.

Jude 1:23 says, *"And others save with fear, pulling them out of the fire; hating even the garment spotted by the flesh."*

Godly jealousy is needed for a man of God to keep his flock. Godly jealousy will cause a man of God to labor in prayer and in the word so that he doesn't lose his flock. Jesus guided the flock jealously. He even offered His life for them so that they will have life (John 17:12).

When a Pastor is driven by Godly Jealousy, he doesn't want anyone in the camp to take his glory from him. He has to be seen as the leader and father of the house.

Paul the apostle was driven by Godly Jealousy to labor for his flock to present them to Christ.

> *"For I am jealous over you with godly jealousy: for I have espoused you to one husband, that I may present you as a chaste virgin to Christ,"*
>
> *(2 Corinthians 11:2)*

Godly jealousy will drive you to raise many laborers in the kingdom. Godly Jealousy will cause you to be fully preoccupied with God's work.

UNGODLY JEALOUSY

When Jealousy is misapplied it becomes ungodly and it ends one up in envy.

> *"Let us not be desirous of vain glory, provoking one another, envying one another,"*
>
> *(Galatians 5:26)*

> *"If any man teach otherwise, and consent not to wholesome words, even the words of our Lord Jesus Christ, and to the doctrine which is according*

to godliness; He is proud, knowing nothing, but doting about questions and strifes of words, whereof cometh envy, strife, railings, evil surmisings, Perverse disputings of men of corrupt minds, and destitute of the truth, supposing that gain is godliness: from such withdraw thyself. But godliness with contentment is great gain,"

(1 Titus 6:3-6KJV)

When you are jealous of a Christian Brother or Sister because of what he or she has, you have not been perfected in the love of God. It's like God being jealous of Himself.

1 Timothy 6:6 says, *"But goodliness with contentment is great gain."*

Everything you need in this life, have already been provided by God.

Ephesians 1:3 says, *"Blessed be the God and Father of our Lord Jesus Christ, who hath blessed us with all spiritual blessings in heavenly places in Christ."*

"According as his divine power hath given unto us all things that pertain unto life and godliness, through the knowledge of him that hath called us to

glory and virtue," (2Peter 1:3KJV)

You have already been given all things that pertain to life and godliness. All you need have been supplied for you. All you need is the knowledge of how to bring it into manifestation.

Ephesians 1:3 speaks of the quantum world where everything you desire exist. It's up to you focus on it. If someone has something that you don't have, it's usually because of their focus in life.

In the quantum world, everything exists; both good and evil.

Whatever you focus on, that thing appears, and almost all the time, your expectations are met. If you therefore want to change your life, you need to change the pictures you are seeing, and the expectations you have.

Understand that all things are yours.

1 Corinthians 3:21 says, *"Therefore let no man glory in men. For all things are yours."*

Verse 22 makes us understand that even the brother who is so blessed is yours. With this understanding, you won't be jealous of anyone again. When jealousy arises in your heart concerning a brother, kill it.

Why Do We Get Jealous Of Another?

1. We get Jealous of someone who is close to us; when we did not support them in their journey, yet they start prospering.

2. When we don't pray for them.

3. When we are with them but our hearts are not with them.

WHEN DO WE GET JEALOUS OF ANOTHER?

1. When we compare ourselves with them and see our inadequacy.

2. When they are preferred by someone we admire, and we feel insignificant in their presence.

3. When they succeed where we failed.

4. When our efforts and labors are trivialized in their presence. Especially when they are more successful.

5. When our weakness is being exposed and we are compared to them.

6. When unexplainable losses occur after we've sown our greatest seeds and yet they seem to harvest with ease after planting same seeds.

So How Do We Kill Ungodly Jealousy?

1. Offer support as much as you can if there is possibility. Be a part of their breakthrough, contribute to their outshining. Decide to serve them.

2. If there's no opportunity to offer physical help, be their intercessor. Support them with prayers. Pray every day for them till all the jealousy disappears. In this way you migrate into another realm. You will be blessed by the thing that you are jealous the person has. When you pray for someone, you create a channel between you and the person for transfer of blessings. As you pray for the person, your heart will be united and you will love each other.

> *"But I say unto you, Love your enemies, bless them that curse you, do good*

to them that hate you, and pray for them which despitefully use you, and persecute you,"

(Matthew 5:44KJV)

CHAPTER NINE

HOW WOMEN DESTROYS THEIR HOMES

"It is better to dwell in a corner of the housetop, than with a brawling woman in a wide house,"

(Proverbs 21:9)

"It is better to dwell in the wilderness, than with a contentious and an angry woman,"

(Proverbs 21:19 KJV)

Every woman must understand that they can be the cause of the calamity in the homes. They may think they did not do anything wrong, but in reality they are the cause of the anger in their homes.

Proverbs 14:1 says, *"Every wise woman buildeth her house: but the foolish plucketh it down with her hands."*

The verses above all have scientific backing. If you want to understand this verse, look up the water experiment by Dr. Masaru Emoto to see how water receives words.

Water is a universal solvent and that whatever you speak over it, it will receive it. Our body is made up of over 75% water, so whatever words you say over us, the water in our body absorbs it.

The mechanism of a woman building her home

Understand that the Bible says through words, the world was framed.

> "Through faith we understand that the worlds were framed by the word of God, so that things which are seen were not made of things which do appear,"
> (Hebrews 11:3)

The woman builds the home by words, not by sweeping or cleaning. Your words must be gracious if you want to build your home. The world speaks the language of frequencies.

When a woman is angry all the time, the water in her body absorbs that frequency. Now when she is nagging and complaining bitterly, the water in her home absorbs that frequency without her knowledge.

Food prepared in love, produces love and unity in the home.

The way to a man's heart is through the stomach. Water is a universal solvent and will receive every word you say over it. Even if your husband doesn't love coming home, you can make him come home all the time by programming the water you use to cook with words of love, and also cooking in love.

The kitchen is the engine of your home. Whatever goes on in the kitchen is what controls the home. If a woman understands this, she will be able to either create a good home or a hell in the home. Woman who love to sing love songs in the kitchen or worship songs while cooking creates a Godly atmosphere in the family. Everyone that eats the food will be filled with love.

A good food is not about the taste, but about the frequency of the food.

Was the food cooked in love? Or it was done in bitterness, complaint and anger?

THINK ON THESE

- The woman builds the home by words, not by sweeping or cleaning.

- Your words must be gracious if you want to build your home.

- The world speaks the language of frequencies.

- The kitchen is the engine of your home. Whatever goes on in the kitchen is what controls the home.

- Food prepared in love, produces love and unity in the home.

- The way to a man's heart is through the stomach. Water is a universal solvent and will receive every word you say over it.

This is a true story

One day I was with a woman in her house. I watched her prepare food in the kitchen. As she cooked, she kept on complaining about why her sister was not helping her. I saw her talking and nagging while cooking. After the food was prepared, we all ate the meal. The next day there was chaos in the house.

Everyone was fighting with the other, but I didn't have that knowledge. Later when I was trying to understand the cause of the fights, I realized it was caused by her anger. The water absorbed it, and was transmitted to everyone that ate the food.

How To Cook With Love

When you are cooking, irrespective of how you are feeling, don't send that feeling to the kitchen. That is the place you create the right ambience for your home.

1. Speak love over your water.
   Say words like "thank you, I love you" "I am lovable; we love; we are happy in this house."

2. Bless the water with joy, love, light, friendliness, and unity.

3. Cook while blessing, singing love songs, or chanting love words. You can chant, "I love you, you love me, we all love one another, we are loved, Jesus loves us, we are happy and blessed in this home."

Food cooked in love will carry the frequency of love. It will taste different from any food in any place. Your husband will never want to eat outside because, he finds proper life-giving food at home.

DIAGNOSING THE CAUSE OF FIGHTING IN THE HOME

If there is always fights in the home, check the attitude of the one cooking your food. He or she could be the cause of it.

If a married man always goes out angry, the problem is coming from his wife. The woman has been cooking while nagging and complaining. However, if the woman, irrespective of the man's attitude will cook her food with love, her husband will turn out to be the most loving man she ever met.

On the other hand, the man should not make the woman bitter, else it will affect him and his prayers will be hindered.

> *"Likewise, ye husbands, dwell with them according to knowledge, giving honour unto the wife, as unto the weaker vessel, and as being heirs together of the grace of*

life; that your prayers be not hindered,"
(1 Peter 3:7 KJV)

REFLECT ON THESE THINGS

- Every woman must understand that they can be the cause of the calamity in the homes.
- The man should not make the woman bitter.

SUMMARY OF FORGIVENESS

1. BE SPECIFIC about what you are forgiving
2. Ask for the help of the Holy Ghost
3. Pray for your enemies

Practicing Forgiveness

1. Sit down straight and close your eyes.
2. Imagine the light from heaven falling on your body.
3. Engage this Light of God, and let it go through you.
4. Connect to the light and with your mind's eye view the darkness around you.
5. Ask yourself, "Who must I forgive?" Their names will come to your mind immediately. Review what they did.

6. Develop empathy for the person.

7. Change the meaning attached to what they did to you, by finding the true meaning. This can be done by pondering over it, and finding a good reason for their actions. You can even ask them questions about their actions in your mind. Listen to the thoughts that arise immediately after the questions, these are the answers. (This may require some help from a mind coach)

8. Mention their name and forgive them completely.

9. Allow the light to illuminate your field and clear the darkness.

10. Imagine the person before you, hug him or her, and let Jesus embrace the two of you, while His light fills the two of you and clear all the darkness completely.

Practice morning forgiveness or Daily forgiveness

This is very important if we want to be free. I was very shocked at myself the number of things that was in me when I scanned my energy field for the first time. I thought forgiving once was enough but every day I get shocked when I scan my energy field. This is because there are some things I never knew I was hurt by until I scanned my energy field. Your mind may be misinterpreting the actions of some people in your head and it will be picked up as a wrong signal. But you need to catch the real meaning attached to it.

REFERENCES

- https://www.womenworking.com/happens-brain-forgive-someone-hurt-emotionally/

- Seeds of Wisdom on Bitterness- Dr. Mike Murdock

Printed in Great Britain
by Amazon